# EGYPTIAN PYRAMIDS!

## ANCIENT HISTORY FOR CHILDREN

Secrets of the Pyramids

## CHILDREN'S ANCIENT HISTORY BOOKS

Left Brain Kids

Educational Books for Children

The Pyramids in Ancient Egypt are considered the most popular pyramid structures in the world even today.

These ancient pyramids were made to serve as tombs for the Pharaohs, including their families. There were more than 130 pyramids discovered in Egypt.

# THE PYRAMID OF DJOSER

It is believed that the first pyramid in Egypt, Pyramid of Djoser, was made in the place called Saqqara, a huge burial ground in the ancient Egypt, near Memphis City.

# THE PYRAMID IN GIZA

It is considered the largest and oldest of all the three pyramids found in Giza Necropolis.

All these pyramids were guarded by what they called Sphinx, which stands in the front of every pyramid in Giza. The Sphinx's body is shaped like a lion, and its head is of the pharaoh.

# THE PYRAMID OF KHUFU

It is known as the oldest among Ancient Wonders in the world. This pyramid is the last that is still mainly intact.

For more than 3800 years, the Great Pyramid of Giza was considered the tallest structure in the whole world that was made by man.

Although it has lost about 33 feet in its height, the pyramid still stands 480 feet above the ground.

The most significant pyramids in Egypt are found in **Giza, Saqqara, Abusir, Dashur, Meidum, Abu Warash, and Lisht.**

Almost all of the pyramids in Egypt are located in west bank of the famous Nile River.

This was done for
easy transportation
of the stones
by boat. These
Egyptian pyramids
usually contain
many passages
and chambers.

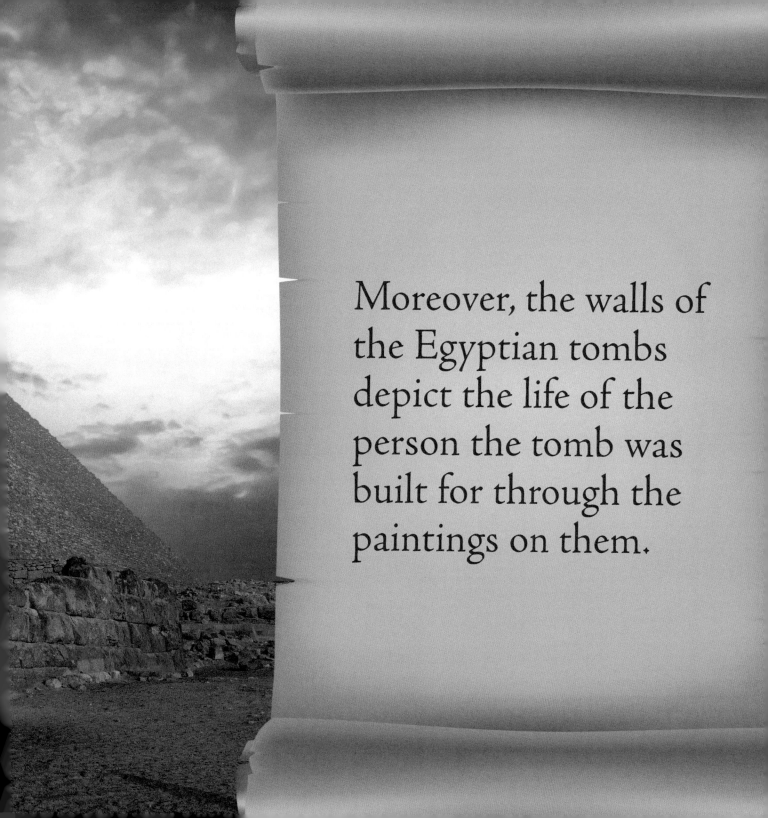

Moreover, the walls of the Egyptian tombs depict the life of the person the tomb was built for through the paintings on them.

These paintings and artifacts allow archaeologists to study the life of archeologists' study of the life of Ancients Egyptians.

The Egyptians used the process of mummification as a way of preserving the bodies before they were placed inside the tombs.

The pyramids were built because the Pharaohs bodies were mummified and placed in the tomb so they could live forever and take their treasures to the afterlife with them. This is because Egyptians believed in the afterlife.

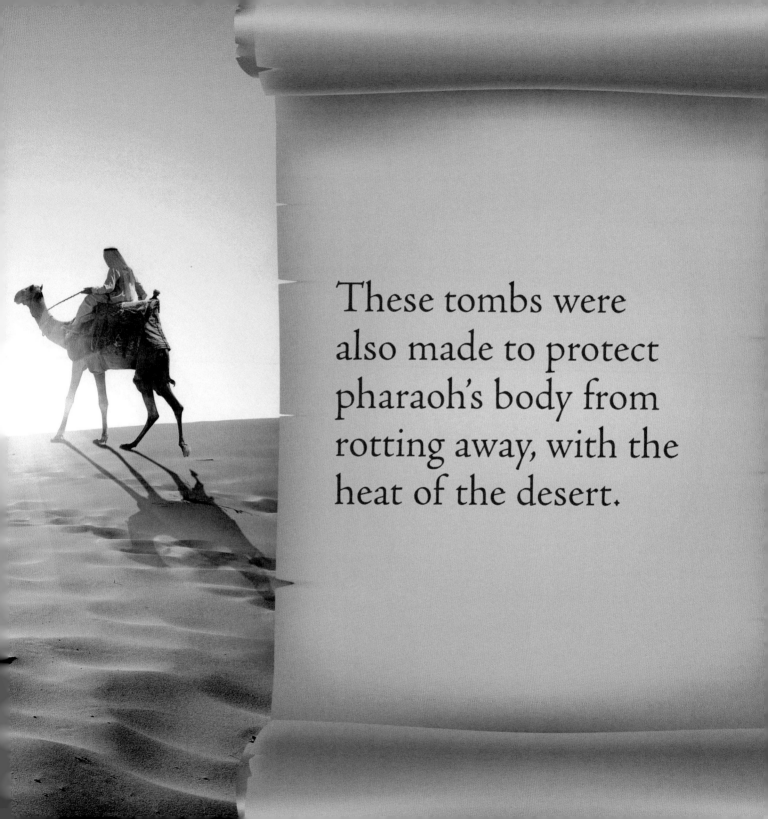

These tombs were also made to protect pharaoh's body from rotting away, with the heat of the desert.

Egyptians paid huge amounts of money for the dead bodies of their loved ones to be preserved properly.

In these tombs, not only bodies were buried but also items that people use on a daily basis and even the expensive jewelery because they believed these were useful in the afterlife.

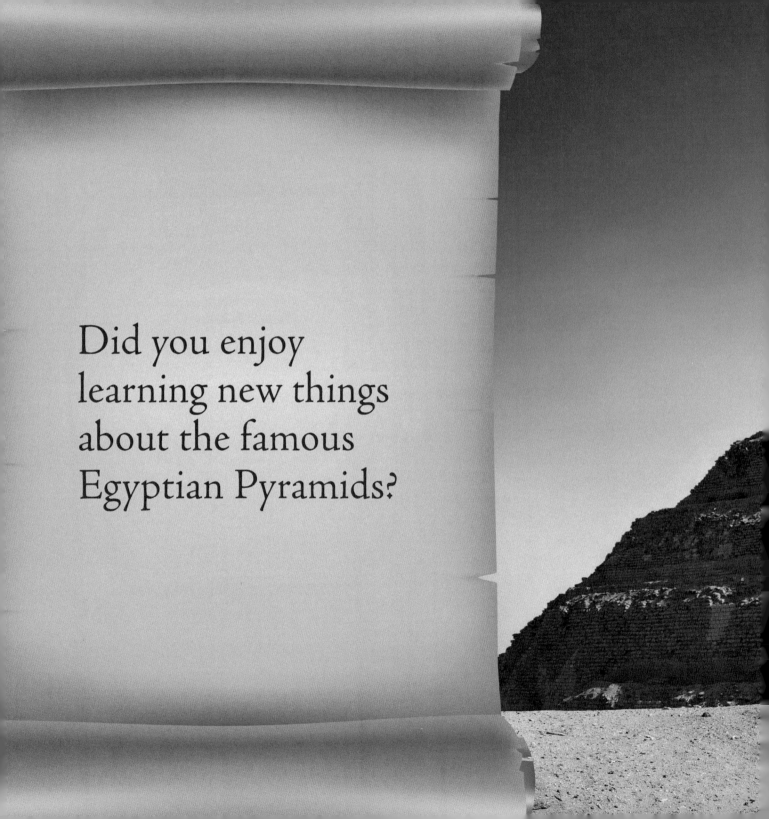

Did you enjoy learning new things about the famous Egyptian Pyramids?

Made in the USA
Coppell, TX
27 June 2021